LEVEL 3

Written by: Barbara Ingham
Series Editor: Melanie Williams

Pearson Education Limited
Edinburgh Gate, Harlow,
Essex CM20 2JE, England
and Associated Companies throughout the world.

ISBN: 978-1-4082-8814-6

This edition first published by Pearson Education Ltd 2013
10
Text copyright © Pearson Education Ltd 2013

The moral rights of the author have been asserted
in accordance with the Copyright Designs and Patents Act 1988

Set in 17/21pt OT Fiendstar
Printed in China
SWTC/10

Acknowledgements

The publisher would like to thank the following for their kind permission to reproduce their photographs:
(Key: b-bottom; c-centre; l-left; r-right; t-top)

Alamy Images: Scott Barclay 19b, Stock Connection Blue 4, Chad Ehlers 19t, Michael Harder 3cl, 5, 23 (e), Hemis 17, Paul Thompson Images 21c, Ladi Kirn 20, Simon Lord 18, Travel Pictures 13r, 23 (c); **Corbis:** Reuters / CORBIS 8, 23 (a), Susana Gonzalez / dpa 10, 23 (d), Lindsay Hebberd 14, Paul C. Pet 11b, title page, Weng Xinyang / Xinhua Press 9, Bobby Yip 3r, 12, 23 (b); **Fotolia.com:** Brad Pict 15; **Getty Images:** Peter Adams 3cr, 6, Education Images / UIG 7; **Photoshot Holdings Limited:** David Robertson 3l, 22; **Shutterstock.com:** ElenaGaak 21 (top), vera-g 21b, Patricia Hofmeester 16, jreika 13l, lrafael 11t
Cover images: *Front:* **SuperStock:** Steve Vidler

All other images © Pearson Education

In some instances we have been unable to trace the owners of copyright material,
and we would appreciate any information that would enable us to do so.

Illustrations: Martin Sanders (Beehive Illustration)

For a complete list of the titles available in the Pearson English Kids Readers series, please go to
www.pearsonenglishkidsreaders.com. Alternatively, write to your local Pearson Education office or to
Pearson English Readers Marketing Department, Pearson Education, Edinburgh Gate, Harlow, Essex CM202JE, England.

Contents

N'cwala, Zambia

Every February in Zambia, there is an important festival called N'cwala. The Ngoni people live in the east of Zambia and celebrate this festival. People dance, clap and sing. The songs are important because they tell a story.

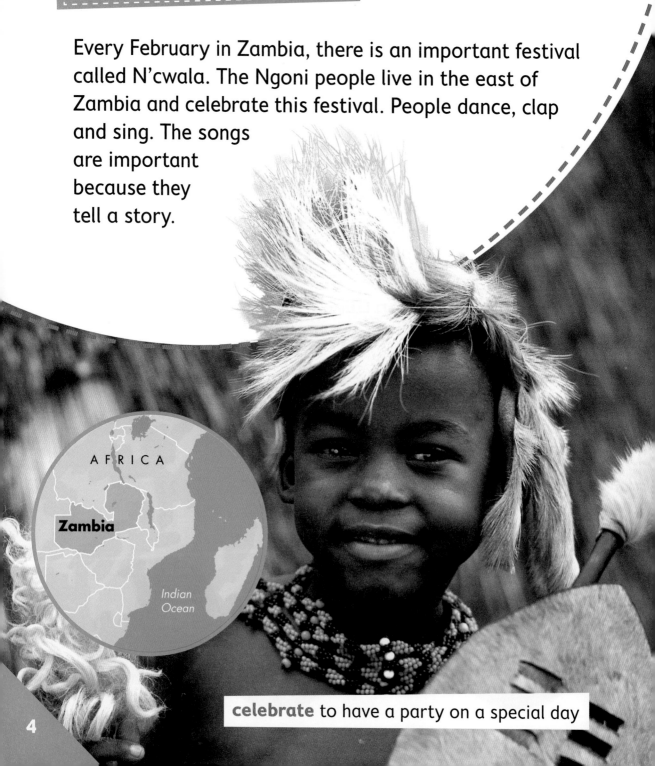

AFRICA

Zambia

Indian Ocean

celebrate to have a party on a special day

warrior dance

At the festival Ngoni boys wear traditional clothes. There is a special warrior dance to loud music. The warrior dance is exciting. Men come from twelve different places and dance in the N'cwala celebrations.

festival a day, or days, of celebration

Festival of the Sahara, Tunisia

This festival is in Tunisia. It happens in the desert in December. The festival celebrates desert people and their culture. It is very hot in the day in the desert but very cold at night.

Mediterranean Sea

Tunisia

A F R I C A

Sahara Desert

It is an exciting festival. In the day, men ride horses and camels. Some men stand on their heads on their horses. It is very dangerous! At night, people read stories and listen to beautiful poems and traditional music.

Rio de Janeiro Carnival, Brazil

The Rio de Janeiro Carnival is in Brazil in February. It is very famous, big and colourful. There are a lot of floats in the Rio street parade.

Brazil

SOUTH
AMERICA

Rio de Janeiro
*Atlantic
Ocean*

float

carnival people wear special clothes and dance in the streets
parade people walk through the streets in celebration

All the people wear beautiful costumes and they dance the samba.

Every year there is a competition, the King of the Carnival. People choose a big Brazilian man from Rio. The name of the King is Momo.

samba a dance

The Day of the Dead, Mexico

The Day of the Dead, El Día de Muertos, is in Mexico from the night of 1st November to 2nd November. It is a happy and colourful festival. It celebrates dead people.

Children wear ghost costumes and masks and parade through the streets.

USA

Mexico

Caribbean Sea

Pacific Ocean

mask

ghost costume

People eat Pan de Muerto, bread in the shape of bones. They also make sugar skulls and decorate them with different colours. Children love them.

Pan de Muerto

Diana

sugar skulls

Carmela

Salvador

decorate to make beautiful

Tet Trung Thu, Vietnam

This festival is in autumn in Vietnam. It is a moon festival. Children walk in the streets and carry lanterns of different shapes. There are candles in the lanterns. They are pretty.

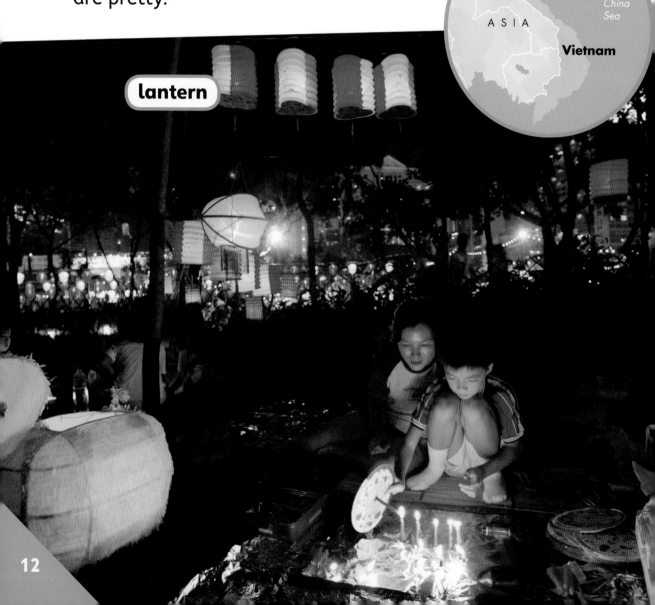

ASIA

South China Sea

Vietnam

lantern

Girls' Day, Japan

In Japan there is a special Girls' Day, Hina Matsuri, on 3rd March. Girls dress in traditional costumes called kimonos. The kimonos have beautiful designs on them. The girls visit friends, drink tea and eat rice cakes.

ASIA

Japan

Pacific Ocean

kimono

Esala Perahera, Sri Lanka

The Esala Perahera happens every year in July and August in the city of Kandy in Sri Lanka. The parade starts at night in the dark. It finishes at midnight.

INDIA

Indian Ocean

Sri Lanka

It is a very old and colourful festival. Many people stand in the streets and watch the parade. Big colourful elephants walk slowly down the streets. On the elephants, there are men in traditional clothes.

Waitangi Day, New Zealand

On 6th February every year New Zealanders celebrate their culture. Maori people open the celebrations with a traditional welcome. This is called the Haka Powhiri.

AUSTRALIA

Pacific Ocean

New Zealand

The Maori warriors' traditional canoe is called a waka.
On Waitangi day, people come and see a very famous
waka. It is called Nga Toki Matawhaorua. It is more
than 70 years old. It can carry more than 100 people!

Australia Day, Australia

Australia Day is on 26th January every year. People celebrate Australia Day with street parades. Many people decorate their faces with different colours. They usually use red, white and blue.

Australia

Pacific Ocean

New Zealand

Many families go and celebrate the day by the sea because Australia is hot in January. Some people like to go sailing. There are always a lot of boats on the water. Families and friends also go to music festivals and listen to all kinds of music.

Midsummer's Eve, Sweden

In Sweden, winter is dark and long and summer is short. In June, people celebrate the long, light summer days on Midsummer's Eve. People dance near the forest and sing songs. It is a happy day.

Sweden

Baltic Sea EUROPE

Girls wear circles of flowers in their hair. They take beautiful flowers from their gardens and the forest. They put the flowers in their beds and they dream of love. On this day they eat special fish, fruit and ice cream.

Hogmanay, Scotland

Hogmanay is the traditional Scottish name for New Year's Eve. The festival happens on 31st December. People visit friends and family. At midnight they say "goodbye" to the old year and "welcome" to the new year with fireworks.

fireworks

Atlantic Ocean

Scotland

North Sea

Northern Ireland

Wales England

Before You Read

❶ Match the pictures to the words.

ghost costume   kimono   carnival   lanterns   warrior dance

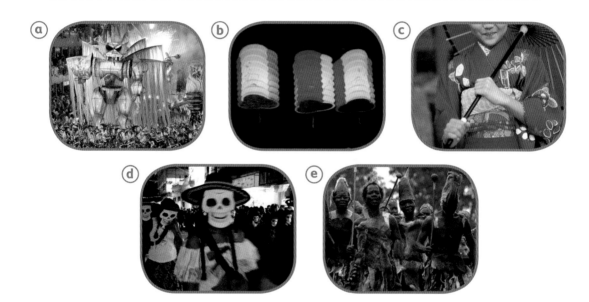

❷ Look in the book. Write the names of the countries correctly.

a aJnap

b dweSne

c riS kaLan

d antSlocd

e ibZmaa

f latrusAai

g oxiMec

h weN leZdana

i lizraB

j siTiaun

k mantiVe

After You Read

1 **Read and write True (T) or False (T).**
  1 There are fireworks at Hogmanay.
  2 Children wear ghost costumes at El Día de Muertos festival.
  3 At the Tet Trung Thu festival there are two important dances.
  4 The Festival of the Sahara happens in March.
  5 Big colourful elephants walk down the streets in the Esala Perahera festival.
  6 It is cold on Australia Day.

2 **Read the sentence and name the festival in the book.**
  1 People eat bread in the shape of bones.
  2 Girls dress in traditional costumes called kimonos.
  3 Boys dress in traditional warrior costumes.
  4 People can see Nga Toki Matawhaorua.
  5 Girls wear circles of flowers in their hair.

3 **Which festival do you like? Write two things about the festival.**